coping with cliques

a workbook to help
girls deal with **gossip,
put-downs, bullying**
& other mean behavior

SUSAN SPRAGUE

Instant Help Books
A Division of New Harbinger Publications, Inc.

Publisher's Note

This publication is designed to provide accurate and authoritative information in regard to the subject matter covered. It is sold with the understanding that the publisher is not engaged in rendering psychological, financial, legal, or other professional services. If expert assistance or counseling is needed, the services of a competent professional should be sought.

Distributed in Canada by Raincoast Books

Copyright © 2008 by Susan Sprague
          Instant Help Books
          A Division of New Harbinger Publications, Inc.
          5674 Shattuck Avenue
          Oakland, CA 94609
          www.newharbinger.com

FSC
Mixed Sources
Product group from well-managed
forests and other controlled sources

Cert no. SW-COC-002283
www.fsc.org
© 1996 Forest Stewardship Council

Cover and text design by Amy Shoup

All Rights Reserved

Printed in the United States of America

ISBN 13: 978-1-57224-654-6

Library of Congress Cataloging-in-Publication Data

Sprague, Susan.
 Coping with cliques : a workbook to help girls deal with gossip, put-downs, bullying, and other mean behavior / Susan Sprague.
   p. cm.
 ISBN-13: 978-1-57224-613-3 (pbk. : alk. paper)
 ISBN-10: 1-57224-613-8 (pbk. : alk. paper)
 1. Teenage girls--Conduct of life. 2. Teenage girls--Life skills guides. 3. Cliques (Sociology) 4. Interpersonal relations in adolescence. 5. Interpersonal conflict in adolescence. I. Title.
 BJ1681.S67 2008
 302.3'408352--dc22
              2008013466

12   11   10

10 9 8 7 6 5 4 3 2 1

First printing

contents

Do you miss out on being invited to the right parties with the "in crowd"? Do your classmates make fun of you on MySpace? Have you been threatened on AIM by someone you don't know? Or are you having trouble finding friends who will stand by you when the most popular girl at school picks on you?

If you've answered yes to any of these questions, know that you're not alone. Adolescence has always been a time when girls draw lines in the sand, and when those lines are drawn, you may feel like you've been left out in the cold. This book will help you know:

- What to do if someone calls you names

- What to do if someone insults you in an e-mail

- What to do if someone makes fun of you online

- How to keep from being the object of gossip

- How to tell when teasing has turned into harassment

- When to ask for help with bullying

- How to deal with hurt feelings and anger

- How to find friends who will be just that—friends

When you finish it, you'll be amazed at how powerful and confident you have become. You'll be able to dish it out without stooping to the level of dirt, and inside you'll have that warm, glowing feeling that comes from being true to what you believe in.

Here's a biggie: In some of the activities, you'll be writing about real people—in your own clique or others. The activities are yours to complete privately, but stuff happens, so take care not to use actual names. You'll avoid hurting anyone else, and you may find that you feel freer to say what you really think.

part 1

sticks and stones can break my bones ...

You've probably heard that old saw before and know how it ends: but names can never hurt me. The truth is, words can hurt. And while they don't physically break bones, they can damage your spirit. Picture this: It's the first day of school. You've chosen your clothes carefully, gotten a new hairstyle, and chatted with your BFF for an hour the night before, filling her in on the details. The next day when you're walking down the hall, BFF takes one look at you and says loudly, "Where'd you get that? The thrift shop?" Everyone looks at you, and you feel your ears burn with humiliation. Before you can answer, the bell rings and you're left there alone.

At times like that, you need to identify what you're feeling instead of heading for the refrigerator or teasing your little brother, or worse, getting on the phone and widening the circle of gossip and outrage. Not until you can identify what you are feeling and how you should react can you go on to become the strong, confident girl you want to be.

1 aww, poor baby— recognizing hurt

starting off ...

Friendship is what makes life super fun and interesting. But what happens when your BFF says something that destroys your self-confidence? Can you reconcile the hurt you're experiencing with the feelings of friendship you have for her? The answer is yes. You can begin the process by freely acknowledging those hurt feelings and not shoving them back down into yourself.

Without friendship, you may wake up in the morning when the alarm goes off and think only of the daily grind of stuff you have to do—yuck. Friendship helps you think about what else will fill the day besides school, homework, and activities. In fact, friends give you that extra push out the door because you know that you will share, giggle, and listen.

But it's not always laughs. Picture a group of friends sitting in the cafeteria, talking about the cute guy in science, when suddenly Brianna says to Emily, "You might have a chance with him if you had hair like Kelly instead of such thin hair." Everyone turns to look at Kelly, whose thick, blonde hair, without a split end in sight, is the envy of the entire school. How can Brianna say that? Just last night Emily slept over at her house, and they stayed up until two o'clock talking about her crush. They've been friends since kindergarten and they've always shared secrets and supported each other.

As Emily sits there, unable to respond, she goes through a torrent of emotions: disbelief, amazement, jealousy, and anger. But she doesn't say anything. When the bell rings, signaling the end of lunch, everyone picks up their backpacks and leaves.

At home after school, Emily is no longer angry, but she feels depressed and sad. She throws herself into her favorite chair in front of the TV and starts watching a soap opera. Its complicated plot is so over the top that by the time dinner rolls around, she's feeling better.

When she thinks about what Brianna said, she suddenly realizes that wherever that remark came from, she'll talk about it with Brianna tomorrow. Without all those emotions roiling around inside, she'll be able to do it.

Pretend you're another one of Emily's friends and you decide to call her after the incident in the cafeteria. Write a dialogue in which you get her to talk about her feelings. These questions can help you get started:

- What kind of solutions do you suggest?

- How does she react?

- Do you think it's better to have her talk to Brianna immediately, or wait? Why?

_____

_____

_____

_____

_____

_____

_____

_____

_____

_____

...and more to do!

Think back to a time when one of your close friends hurt you, either intentionally or accidentally.

Describe where you were.

_____

_____

_____

_____

What was the first feeling you had?

_____

_____

_____

_____

What did you say?

_____

_____

_____

_____

What did you do when you were alone?

_____

_____

_____

_____

How did you feel about the incident the next day?

_____

_____

_____

_____

_____

_____

_____

2 catch those feelings—recognizing sadness

starting off ...

Whether deliberately or unintentionally, other girls sometimes make chance remarks that upset you. Often you don't know what to make of these verbal jabs, yet you're left with feelings of sadness that you might try to ignore. After all, friends are never supposed to hurt each other's feelings, right? Wrong! Whether it's a girl from another clique or one of your own friends, you've been subjected to insults. It's important to recognize what you are feeling instead of denying it. Admit what it is and you're on the first step to dealing with it.

It's Friday night, and Shauna is at Jessie's house. It makes Donald Trump's Mar-a-Lago look like a dump! As they say in the car ads, it's fully loaded: a home theater, an in-ground swimming pool, and four bathrooms. Even Jessie's room looks like a magazine picture, with a canopied bed, window seat, and walk-in closet.

Shauna? Well, she has to share a bedroom with her bratty eight-year-old sister—and she's lucky to even have a house since her parents divorced.

As she stands gaping at the aqua and brown decor, she says wistfully, "What a fab room. Did you get to pick out the colors and shop for the accessories?"

Jessie just looks at her and says, "No, Mom uses the decorating firm in town." She pauses slightly and then adds, "It must be hard for you to have to share your room, but I guess it's nice that you got to decorate it with your mom's old beanbag chairs."

The look on her face is sympathetic, but the words shoot through Shauna. Jessie is her friend. They've been in school together since third grade, and Shauna has listened and supported her through really tough times. Now this?

Face it. Jessie may be her real true friend, but what she said has hurt Shauna and made her sad.

On the lines below, write about one of your own experiences with a friend who unintentionally made you feel sad. To start you off, here are some questions:

- What did you do about your sad feelings?

- Were you open about them? Why or why not?

- Did you trust your friend with talking about your feelings? Why or why not?

- If you had to experience the moment all over again, would you react differently?

_____

_____

_____

_____

_____

_____

_____

_____

_____

_____

_____

...and more to do!

The tables have turned. Write about a time that you unintentionally made one of your best friends sad. How did she react? How did you respond and why?

_____

_____

_____

_____

_____

_____

_____

_____

_____

_____

_____

_____

_____

_____

starting off ...

It can be hard for girls to admit that they are angry. After all, remember what your mother says when your brothers fight: "Boys will be boys." Yet when you fight with your sister, she says, "You ought to know better." People might think it's okay for boys to express their anger more openly than girls do, but that's beside the point: we all know that everyone does gets angry at one time or another. What happens when you get angry? You might feel your body tighten up or your face flush. You might feel grouchy with everyone without knowing exactly why. You may not even want to be with your friends. No matter how anger affects you, recognizing its symptoms can make it easier to deal with.

Jennifer and her friend Tara both want the lead part in the school play. Another friend, Jessica, tells her that Tara is bragging that her own tryout was way better than Jennifer's. Inwardly, Jennifer is in a state of disbelief, even though there's a small part of her that suspects Tara may be right. She keeps telling herself over and over that what Tara thinks really doesn't affect their friendship—they're both just trying for the same part, that's all. As she thinks about it, her stomach begins to hurt.

And then there's Ashley. Her group of friends—her clique—are all friends for a reason. They like the same music, the same movies, hanging out at the mall, and truth be known, sitting together in the cafeteria is often the best part of their day. But when Erin makes fun of the boy Ashley has a crush on in front of everyone else, Ashley feels like crying. How can Erin do that? She knows full well how much Ashley likes him. Suddenly, all Ashley can think about is diving into a pint of ice cream.

Think about times when you were upset by something another person said to you. Put a check mark next to each reaction you have had at those times.

☐ Your face turned red.

☐ You sighed.

☐ You burst into tears.

☐ You got a headache.

☐ You felt detached.

☐ Your stomach hurt.

☐ You felt like everything around you was unreal.

☐ You felt restless and agitated.

Surprise! If you've ever had any of these reactions in response to a stressful situation, what you've experienced is probably anger, which is normal. And if you haven't had any of these reactions, the next time you find yourself in a tense situation, take careful note of what you're feeling.

...and more to do!

What are you likely to do when a friend makes you angry?

☐ 1. Go home and take a nap.

☐ 2. Tell yourself it doesn't matter what your friend thinks.

☐ 3. Try to laugh it off in front of the clique.

☐ 4. Hit your sister or brother.

☐ 5. Tell your friend that you're angry, and why.

☐ 6. Eat a huge bowl of ice cream.

☐ 7. Write a letter to your friend and then rip it up.

☐ 8. Yell at your parents.

☐ 9. Kick your dog.

If you've actually done 4, 8, or 9, it's time to rethink how you react to anger. Take a long, deep breath to calm yourself down.

If you've done 1 or 6 most of the time, yeah, ice cream is tasty and a nap after stress is good, but think about this: are you working through the anger or are you displacing it with another activity?

If you've done 2 or 3 more frequently, you might be in danger of denying your anger. Consider letting it out in a more constructive fashion.

If you've always done 5 or 7, you've come a long way toward recognizing that you can't let angry feelings fester. The exact moment often isn't the right time to respond, but once you have full command over yourself, you can approach the person. Or if the issue is small, write a letter and pour out all those feelings. Then tear it up. You'll feel the stress and tension start to flow right out of you.

4 teasing: the good, the bad, and the unintended

starting off ...

All teens tease. If you have a brother or a sister who just loves to get a rise out of you, you know that for sure. (And you know what the sibs can do to your equilibrium!) In fact, you've probably teased your friends when you felt ill at ease, when you liked a certain someone who shall remain nameless, or when you felt so comfortable with your friends that teasing seemed okay. When teasing is good, the person being teased knows that she can ask the other person to stop. And what happens when the teasing goes too far? If your BFF occasionally gets carried away, well, you may be able to chalk it up to the moment. But what about when someone in your clique wants to put a girl in her place? She'll usually manage to press a hot button or sore point, and the result is a painful sting to the other girl.

1. Mandy saw Lakeisha walking to the bus stop and waved her over. "Do you want to go to the movies tonight? My mom said she would drop us off."

   Lakeisha was excited. "Sure, let's see the new Nancy Drew movie over at the Odeon."

   Mandy pulled a face. "And maybe you should buy some lollipops and a jump rope to take with you."

   Lakeisha tapped her on the arm. "And I'll take some diapers for you, girlfriend."

2. Lakeisha and Mandy saw Paige, a girl in another clique, waiting in line to see the latest action film. Paige spotted them and said loudly to the girl who was standing next to her, "Well, look whose parents actually let them out of the house. Do you have a permission slip to get into a PG-13 movie too?"

3. After the movie, Lakeisha and Mandy headed to the ice cream shop. When they got there, they couldn't decide on a flavor. "How about chocolate fudge?" suggested Lakeisha.

"Nah, maybe I shouldn't have any," said Mandy.

"That's right," replied Lakeisha. "Everyone should lose at least ten pounds."

Mandy bristled. "Are you saying that I need to lose weight?"

Lakeisha looked at the expression on her friend's face and quickly said, "Forget it. It's just something stupid my mom always says when she's trying on bathing suits."

Tell whether you think each statement below is true or false, and then explain your choice.

Lakeisha and Mandy aren't the best of friends because Mandy thinks Lakeisha has terrible taste in movies.

_____

_____

_____

Paige probably made Mandy and Lakeisha laugh with her humorous remark about getting into the movie with a permission slip.

_____

_____

_____

Lakeisha secretly feels that Mandy should lose ten pounds.

_____

_____

_____

Lakeisha made the remark about ten pounds because she wanted to make her friend laugh.

_____

_____

_____

_____

Lakeisha didn't mind the remark Mandy made about her juvenile taste in movies because she dished it right back to Mandy.

_____

_____

_____

_____

...and more to do!

It's important to be able to tell the difference between good teasing and bad teasing, both intentional and unintentional. Remember, it's what you feel that will give you a clue to what type it is.

Which paragraph is an example of good teasing? Why?

_____

_____

_____

Which paragraph is an example of unintentional bad teasing? Why?

_____

_____

_____

Which paragraph is an example of bad teasing? Why?

_____

_____

_____

Write about a time when you teased a friend in your clique. What kinds of things did you say? How did she respond?

_____

_____

_____

Write about a time when someone from another clique teased you. What was your first reaction? Was it effective? Why or why not? What could you have done differently?

_____

_____

_____

Write about a time when a friend teased you and you felt hurt. What did you say to her? Did she apologize? If so, how did you feel then?

_____

_____

_____

the endless game of telephone

5

starting off ...

Gossip is a slippery slope. Sometimes a casual conversation about others can become like an episode from tabloid TV, and all the starring characters are people who aren't there. Hey, it's harmless, isn't it? The answer to that depends on how it affects you and the people you're gossiping about. In fact, it might well be the first step toward bullying.

The group is hanging out in Meghan's bedroom, talking about the latest issue of *Seventeen*, and the next minute the discussion veers off into what Kara, Meghan's BFF and the most popular girl in school, said to Emma, the new student. Suddenly Meghan can't help but feel a teensy bit uncomfortable. After all, she kind of likes Emma, and Kara can be bossy. But soon she's dragged into the whole stew of the gossip dish.

So what difference does it make? Well, if she agrees, loudly or silently, with her BFF's announcement that Emma is a dork, the next time she sees Emma in the hall, she might not be as friendly to her. Pretty soon, the whole clique of girls, led by Kara, will be silently walking past Emma. And what about how Emma feels? She's probably wondering what she did wrong, except maybe wear the wrong style of jeans.

Read the following scenarios and then answer the questions after each one.

Scenario 1

"So what if she's new," Kara said to her circle of friends. "She just comes into the school as if she freakin' owns the place."

"Yeah," Meghan agreed.

The other girls nodded as they all watched the object of Kara's tirade lean against her locker and chat with Ryan, the center of the basketball team.

"Look at her," Kara sputtered, as Emma twisted a lock of her hair around her finger and laughed at one of Ryan's lame jokes.

"Yeah, she definitely thinks she's all that," Meghan said.

How would you describe this gossip? Is it malicious or not? Tell why.

_____

_____

_____

In your opinion, do conceited girls deserve to be talked about, as long as they don't know? Can you think of any way this might be harmful?

_____

_____

_____

What are the girls' remarks motivated by?

_____

_____

_____

Scenario 2

"Did you get a view of her jeans?" Kara said as Emma walked by. "Didn't she look in the mirror this morning?"

Meghan giggled. "Maybe she bought them five pounds ago."

All the girls burst into laughter, and Emma, at her locker, glanced at them nervously.

Ryan walked by at that moment and stopped to chat with Emma. "Say, new girl, what's up?" he asked.

She smiled and said, "Nothing much. I'm not feelin' the love from that bunch over there, though."

Across the hallway, Kara said, "She is so disgusting. She looks like Britney Spears on a bad day with that dye job."

Is the tone of this gossip session the same as in scenario 1? Why or why not?

_____

_____

_____

Is gossip negative only if the person being talked about overhears? Explain your answer.

_____

_____

_____

How can gossip negatively affect a person's reputation?

_____

_____

_____

Scenario 3

Kara looked at Emma across the hallway and then slammed her locker. "What a skank," she said to her group of friends in a semilow voice.

Meghan was the first to reply. "You can tell she thinks she's something, with those way-tight jeans."

Just then Ryan sauntered up to Emma. "What's up? Girls not talking to you?" he asked.

Emma flushed. "I don't know. Oh well, I don't care, really."

Across the hallway, Kara said loudly, "Do much shopping, Emma, where you come from?"

Emma turned away from Ryan and asked, "Who, me?" Meghan laughed.

"It doesn't look like it. From the way your clothes fit, it looks as though it's been at least two years."

All the girls burst into giggles—except for Emma, who grabbed her books, slammed her locker door, and ran down the hallway.

How would you describe this gossip? Is it malicious or not? Tell why.

_____

_____

_____

Why do you think Ryan is friendly to Emma? Does it help the situation? Why or why not?

_____

_____

_____

What should Emma do? Does ignoring the taunts help or hurt her in this situation?

_____

_____

_____

...and more to do!

Write about a time when you participated in a gossip session like the ones above. What were your emotions?

_____

_____

_____

_____

_____

_____

_____

_____

_____

_____

_____

_____

6   when the gossip tables turn

starting off ...

When the gossip mill gets going, it can suddenly switch into high gear and get mean and nasty in no time at all, so it's important to be careful about those gossip sessions. And remember, what your friends in the clique say about you, they just might say behind your back. Once that starts, you never know when the tone will shift and you'll become the butt of their verbal jabs.

Here's Kara in action again. Read the following scenarios and then answer the questions after each one.

Scenario 1

Kara looked at her best friend, Meghan, as she was getting her books out of the locker.

"God, Meghan," she said. "You're such a nerd!"

Meghan bristled. "What do you mean? I have to do my homework, ya know."

Kara sighed. "That's what I mean, girlfriend. You're so obvious about it, taking every single textbook home every night. Everything has to be just so organized and cutesy-wutesy, even your clothes! Just look at you—all matchey-matchey, Little Miss Perfect."

The clique of girls giggled at this last flourish, while Meghan inwardly cringed.

Does this count as teasing, gossip, or bullying? Explain your choice.

_____

_____

_____

What's the difference between the three?

_____

_____

_____

Is Kara aware that she's being hurtful to Meghan's face?

_____

_____

_____

How should Meghan handle this?

_____

_____

_____

Will Kara's behavior stop if Meghan says nothing?

_____

_____

_____

How might the previous gossip sessions about Emma have contributed to Meghan's dilemma?

_____

_____

_____

Scenario 2

Kara caught up with Meghan as she was hurrying away from her locker. "What's the matter? Can't you take a little teasing now and then?" she asked.

A tight-lipped Meghan turned around. "It didn't feel like teasing. It felt like a full-on assault!"

The other girls silently stared at the floor.

Kara looked coldly at Meghan. "Listen, you little freakin' weirdo, I don't have any idea why I tolerate you. Go home and blow your nose." With that parting shot, she turned on her heels.

Meghan walked home slowly, thinking to herself that she shouldn't have overreacted. After all, how many times had she joined in similar sessions, saying snide things about people just loud enough so they could hear? But this time, the remarks were about her. The next day it would be all over school, just as she thought she had lost her rep as the biggest goody-two shoes of all time.

When she got home, there was a message from Kara on the answering machine: "Hey, goof, sorry about all that. Are we going study for the geography test at the library tonight? Let me know." Click.

Meghan stared at the machine. What had just happened? Did this mean that everything was okay between them? She stood in her living room, a mass of confusion, sadness, and anger.

Why do you think Kara suddenly turned on Meghan? Was she justified?

_____

_____

_____

Describe Kara's relationship with Meghan. Do you think she's jealous? Why or why not?

_____

_____

_____

Does Kara's apology on the answering machine suffice? Why or why not?

_____

_____

_____

How could Meghan have reacted to Kara's taunts? How would you have reacted?

_____

_____

_____

Should Meghan continue to be friends with Kara? If so, what should change in the friendship? What needs to happen for this change to take place?

_____

_____

_____

...and more to do!

How do you think a girl can avoid gossip in casual goofing around with friends?

_____

_____

_____

How can you avoid being the butt of gossip?

_____

_____

_____

When is it okay to stick up for yourself?

_____

_____

_____

Is it better to stick up for yourself when you're angry or when you're calm? Why?

_____

_____

_____

stand up and be counted 7

starting off ...

In any situation where you are being manipulated or verbally browbeaten, have a little backbone; a spine is a good thing when the gossip tables have turned on you, whether by another clique or by friends within your own clique. If it happens with one of your own so-called friends, just remember that a friend is not the boss of you. She's not in charge of whether you feel good about yourself. Sure, she can slip occasionally, but when she alternates between super niceness and downright Cruella Deville nastiness, it's time for you to take action and defend yourself.

For each of the following situations, write a dialogue starring you—yes, you—and how you stand up for yourself.

Situation 1

You and your friends have a huge English project due the next day, and you are all at the library working on your papers. You've slaved over this paper, but after you turn it in, your English teacher confronts you. The verdict? He accuses you and your BFF of passing in the very same paper. You decide to speak to your friend.

_____

_____

_____

_____

_____

_____

_____

_____

_____

_____

_____

_____

_____

Situation 2

You and your BFF like, really like, the same boy. You accidentally overhear him say that he can't stand her. To complicate things a little more, you suddenly realize that there's a girl-ask-boy dance coming up, and she plans to ask him. What are you going to do?

_____

_____

_____

_____

_____

_____

_____

_____

_____

_____

_____

_____

Situation 3

The most popular clique of alpha girls has been passing around rumors like cooties. Today, they were passing notes about you. What do you say to the ringleader after school?

_____

_____

_____

_____

_____

_____

_____

_____

_____

_____

_____

_____

_____

...and more to do!

Answer these questions:

Does standing up for yourself mean that you need to yell or say insulting things?

_____

What does standing up for yourself mean?

_____

_____

_____

Decide which of these phrases is the most effective way to begin explaining, without being judgmental, how another person's behavior has affected you. Then tell why you chose that phrase.

- No offense, but ...

- How come you always ...

- How dare you say that ...

- When you say that, I feel ...

_____

_____

_____

_____

_____

8 when you're the bully—oh no!

starting off ...

You're thinking that you could never be the bully. Oh no, everyone likes you. Or maybe they don't like you and they've teased you in the past, but you would never ever do to them what they did to you. Well, guess again. After all, you're only human. If a situation presents itself, wouldn't you be the slightest bit tempted? You probably would. But resist that temptation, or else the gossip-bully syndrome will go on and on, knocking everyone down and making school utterly and totally poisonous. You can choose to respond in a way that will make it stop.

Situation 1

The most popular clique in school has suddenly shut out a girl who used to be right in there with them. This girl has practically tortured you all through middle school, and you and your friends nicknamed her "Living Nightmare." Now that you have a chance to dish, you see her in the hallway.

Write a scenario in which you act out all your revenge fantasies.

_____

_____

_____

_____

_____

_____

_____

_____

_____

_____

_____

_____

Now write a scenario in which you turn the other cheek because you know what it's like to be bullied.

_____

_____

_____

_____

_____

_____

_____

_____

_____

_____

Situation 2

You find out that the most popular girl in school has gotten awfully close to that cute guy in her math class, and the object of her affections has been spreading a rumor throughout school about what they've done. When someone whispers it to you in study hall, what do you say?

Write a scenario in which you respond to the whispered gossip.

_____

_____

_____

_____

_____

_____

_____

_____

_____

_____

_____

_____

...and more to do!

Reread all three of your scenarios. Which one is truest to the person you know yourself to be? Tell why.

_____

_____

_____

_____

_____

_____

_____

_____

_____

_____

_____

9   are you part of the problem?

---

starting off ...

Language is powerful. For example, when you tell your little sister that she needs to wipe her nose, you might say, "Go blow your disgusting boogers, brat!" Or maybe you are the model of politeness and simply say, "Please blow your nose." Most words have a negative or positive **connotation**, which is the effect that they have on people. Generally, people will remember what you've called them or how you've described them, especially when it's in a teasing or an angry way. In a sense, you are naming them with the words that you choose, whether you intend to or not.

Perhaps you've been the brunt of someone else's teasing. Did that teasing occur in a vacuum? In other words, did one of your friends just come up to you and say, "You're definitely a wide load yourself"? Probably not. She might have said it in response to your teasing jab of, "Don't take the last cookie. You certainly don't need it, thunder thighs!"

Teasing is almost always part of an exchange, but if you want problem teasing to stop, you have to own up to your own use of hurtful words. Your task in this activity is to recognize the words that signal teasing—the naming of people or actions in a negative fashion.

Match the following words to their meanings:

Wacko	A computer whiz
Nerd	A lazy person
Screwup	Someone who's crazy
Geek	Someone who's flighty and frivolous
Klutz	A brainiac
Slacker	A girl with no morals
Airhead	A clumsy person
Skank	Someone who always messes things up

Now choose one of these words and write about a time someone used it to describe you. How did it make you feel?

_____

_____

_____

_____

_____

_____

_____

_____

...and more to do!

Just for kicks and giggles, write two paragraphs. In the first paragraph, use teasing words to tell your friend that her skirt is ugly and that she should fix her messy hair before she goes to the dance.

_____

_____

_____

_____

_____

_____

In the second paragraph, gently tell your friend that the skirt she's wearing is unflattering and that her hair needs brushing.

_____

_____

_____

_____

_____

_____

Now reread both paragraphs. Which one would have the result you would want for your friend? Why?

_____

_____

_____

_____

_____

_____

_____

_____

_____

_____

10 teasing—how to catch yourself in time

starting off ...

When you're smack in the middle of a dish session, letting off steam about parental units, boys, teachers, bratty sisters, and disgusting brothers, it's easy to turn the dish to teasing each other. Face-to-face teasing can be more fun than talking about people because you get an immediate reaction. Sometimes this teasing is a way of being friends. But at other times, you might find yourself tempted to tease friends under of the guise of "just kidding." Teasing can be a mask for simmering emotions—for example, how you really feel about the latest addition to your clique with her Kate Spade handbag and daily new outfits.

Read these examples of teasing. Put a check mark next to teasing that is acceptable and an X next to teasing that has gone too far and might be considered hurtful.

☐ Oh, it's you! You know, we could tell by the rose-garden smell.

☐ So how many frosted doughnuts do you eat in a day? Hmm ... that must be why you're such a wide load.

☐ I can't believe you're going to wear leggings and boots to the mixer. Where'd you get your fashion sense—from the North Pole?

☐ What's up, nerd-face? Got anything going on tonight? Oh, I forgot—you have a date with the library.

☐ You better watch what you say, especially when you answer questions in algebra; you're starting to sound like a math geek.

☐ When you sing, you sound just like a whale with diarrhea.

☐ It's your turn at bat, so the rest of us can just take a nap.

☐ There's your crush, old pepperoni-face. Why don't you go sit down next to him and chat him up? I'm sure he'll think he's died and gone to heaven.

☐ I'm so glad we didn't have to sit next to your little sister at the concert. I can't believe you're from the same planet, let alone the same family. You're so cool, and she's such a fat little moron. Of course, you could always take a page from her fashion book and then you'd fit in with the family.

...and more to do!

Reread the examples. Do any ring a bell with you? Have you had your BFF say something similar to you? How did it make you feel? How did you react?

_____

_____

_____

_____

_____

_____

Write about a time when you and your friends were in the middle of a dish session and the teasing got out of hand. Describe the kind of teasing words you each used. What was your reaction? The reaction of the others?

_____

_____

_____

_____

_____

_____

gossip words and how to spot 'em 11

starting off ...

Dishing with your girlfriends means that, if you're not careful, the chat can quickly tip over into a "he said, she said" scenario. By itself, that isn't so bad. But when the conversation slides down into "God, his zits are as huge as pepperonis," you know that you're swimming in the River Mean. But how did you get there, you ask yourself. The truth is, you can't remember. What you need to work on now is identifying those phrases and words that are signals for a malicious dish of gossip, so you can learn to spot the danger signals.

Fill in the following sentences with phrases or words that signal impending gossip. Be as inventive as you want.

When we got to the dance, _____ was there, holding a
(person's name)

_____ and looking like a _____.
(adjective + noun)   (adjective + noun)

When _____ asked me to dance,
(person's name)

I _____ three times. Then I told him he was so _____.
(verb)   (adjective).

At the dance, I can't stand it when people _____ , especially when
(verb)

it's someone who's _____.
(adjective)

When that _____walked in, I
(adjective + noun)

_____ so _____ that I _____.
(verb)   (adverb)   (verb)

Just then, I whispered to my friend, "Don't _____ anyone, but
                                                      (verb)

I just heard that _____ is _____
                              (person's name)   (verb that ends in "-ing")

tomorrow. Isn't that _____?"
                                    (adjective)

I hate girls like _____, who love to _____
                          (person's name)   (verb)

and _____.
              (verb)

Don't take offense, but I was just in the _____
                                                        (name of a place)

and I saw _____
                        (girl's name)

_____. Isn't she your new BFF?
       (verb that ends in "-ing")

Pinky-swear, but did you see that _____ Tanya at
                                                  (adjective)

the movies? She looked totally _____ wearing that
                                            (adjective)

_____
              (adjective + noun).

I can't believe that _____ would actually
                                    (person's name)

_____ and then _____ about it.
          (verb)   (verb)

When I _____ want to talk about
                          (adverb)

_____, I Sometimes feel
                      (phrase)

_____ about myself.
              (adjective)

...and more to do!

Of the sentences you completed, choose the three you think are most likely to start the River Mean flowing. Rewrite each so that you and your friends don't drown!

_____

_____

_____

_____

_____

_____

_____

_____

_____

_____

_____

_____

_____

12 telling the parental units without making them freak out

starting off ...

Most of the time you're perfectly capable of solving your own problems, especially with your friends, but once in a while, you may need a little help from your parents. What if you're the constant object of teasing and malicious gossip? It can be helpful to have an adult perspective on the situation, especially when the teasing is out of control. The problem is how to tell them so they don't go over the top.

If you blurt out your situation like a drama queen, with adjectives describing every single emotion you've had for the last five months, you'll probably just end up getting your parents as upset as you are. And while it might feel good to get all those feelings off your chest, consider the cost of making everyone concerned.

Instead, think about telling them in terms of the result that you would like: a solution to your problem. Mentally list the facts of what's happened to you. Stick to the details and then at the end, tell them how the situation makes you feel. Whatever you do, don't suggest that they call the parents of your torturer, even if the torturer is your friend. Instead, ask them to help you devise some options for dealing with the teasing and the gossip.

Rate each approach on its effectiveness for telling parents about a troublesome situation. Use 1 for the least effective and 5 for the most effective. Then explain why you chose each rating.

Mom, could you get off the phone right now? Rachel and Sara are putting notes in my locker saying that I'm a loser, honestly!

_____

_____

_____

Mom, could you help with a problem I've been having? How do I get revenge on Rachel and Sara without getting into trouble at school? You wouldn't believe what they've been doing!

_____

_____

_____

Mom, do you remember Rachel and Sara? They've decided that they're not going to be friends with me, and they've been so mean. I don't want to go to school anymore. Can you home-school me, please?

_____

_____

_____

Mom, Rachel and Sara have been leaving notes in my locker for about two weeks. The notes have comments about how I look and how stupid I am. What am I going to do? My life is over!

_____

_____

_____

Mom, Rachel and Sara have been leaving notes in my locker for about two weeks. The notes are full of obscenities. I've tried telling them to stop it a couple of times, but they just laughed and walked away. I'm starting to feel left out of activities, and I think word has spread around the school. Can you help me think of what to do next?

_____

_____

_____

...and more to do!

Now write your own dialogue asking one of your parents to help you with a problem involving teasing or malicious gossip. How do you think they would react?

_____

_____

_____

_____

_____

_____

_____

_____

_____

_____

_____

part 2

*

skank or little miss perfect?

What's your reputation like? How do others look at you? Are they judging you by the kind of shoes you wear or the music you listen to, or are they looking at the kind of people you hang out with? You know what they say: beauty is only skin deep. But did "they" ever wake up with a gigantic pimple on their face the morning of the homecoming dance? Or did "they" ever look in the full-length mirror and suddenly see five extra pounds of jelly belly hanging over the jeans? Take the other girls in your clique: are they lining their eyes with black eyeliner and checking out leather belts for their Goth image, or are they coordinating their shoes and T-shirts with the latest spring colors?

In this section, you'll be able to figure out those stereotypes that you've heard bandied about, and you'll find out that the new girl with the torn jeans and shock of purple hair probably isn't the reject that the popular clique claims. Or even better, when you're the new kid on the block and word gets around that you're a nerd just because you spent last Tuesday studying in the library, you'll be able to hold your own at the next dance and be the first one on the dance floor, demonstrating your moves.

13 dream girl vs. reject girl

From the following list, choose words that describe your idea of dream girls and reject girls. Write your choices in the appropriate column on page 56. You can choose words that describe each girl physically, but also select words that describe her personality and character. Remember, it's the whole package that counts, inside and out.

indifferent	selective	intolerant
creative	smart	sexy
hot	kind	chatty
outgoing	introverted	extroverted
pretty	homely	quiet
serious	studious	insecure
conceited	snobbish	athletic
malicious	stupid	stylish
wild	conservative	religious
peaceful	tolerant	blonde
dark haired	tall	curly haired
short	heavy	petite
thin	well dressed	hyperactive
calm	aggressive	controlling
spoiled	poorly dressed	

activity 13 ✱ dream girl vs. reject girl

Dream Girl	Reject Girl

...and more to do!

Describe how you view yourself both physically and emotionally. What qualities do you see yourself as having? What are some qualities you don't have? Do you feel that these qualities are important? Why or why not?

_____

_____

_____

_____

_____

_____

_____

_____

_____

_____

_____

_____

In the box on the left, draw a picture of yourself. Yeah, so you may not be an artist, but just sketch out how you see yourself. Then, on the right, draw a picture of yourself doing something that shows how you typically deal with people. Are you aloof and reserved? Bubbly and extroverted? Kind and caring?

mirror, mirror on the wall ... 14

---

starting off ...

In creating your list of dream-girl and reject-girl qualities, you must have had a regular vision of these two rolling around inside your brain. At the top of your list you may have started off with a purely physical description, before you got to the more important traits, such as kindness to small children and old people! What you want to do is examine the stereotypes that you've built in your mind and figure out what qualities are truly important.

Reread your list of dream-girl qualities and decide if each quality is important and has value for you. Explain your reasons.

_____

_____

_____

_____

_____

_____

_____

_____

Now look at the qualities you've listed for the reject girl and decide which ones have value for you and why.

_____

_____

_____

_____

_____

_____

_____

_____

_____

_____

_____

_____

...and more to do!

Consider the following: Is it possible to be a reject girl, yet still have some qualities of the dream girl? Why or why not? Can you give an example of someone who embodies both? How is she perceived by your clique? Is their perception fair? Why or why not?

_____

_____

_____

_____

_____

_____

_____

_____

_____

_____

_____

_____

_____

15 what's to hate?

starting off ...

Perception is everything—not just what you can see physically, but what you perceive with your mind. What one person may see as a liability, another might see as an asset. Often, you tend to look at others in terms of what you yourself don't have. And once you start doing that, you have a recording of what's wrong with you playing over and over in your head.

Latoya has a bubbly, outgoing personality. She radiates energy and magnetism. Her best friend, Natasha, is quiet, and truth be told—she'll admit it—shy.

They are great friends, yet Latoya secretly wishes she had some of Natasha's stick-to-itiveness. Grown-ups seem to trust Natasha more than Latoya because she always does what she says she's going to do. She's on the student council every school year, she's organizing a food drive for the needy, and she's spearheading an antilitter campaign for the school. Well, you get the picture. Latoya thinks that at times, she herself can't keep two thoughts inside her head, let alone get the whole school into action.

On the other hand, Natasha secretly envies the vivacious Latoya. At every party they go to, Latoya lightens the mood as soon as she enters the room. Latoya will stop and speak to total strangers, share a giggle, and make people smile. In class, whenever Latoya raises her hand, teachers smile and call on her just because she's Latoya and her answer will be funny.

Are people likely to think of Latoya as reject girl or dream girl? What would they think about Natasha? What do you think these judgments would be based on?

_____

_____

_____

_____

What are Natasha's qualities, both (air quotes here!) reject and dream? What are Latoya's qualities, both (air quotes here, too!) reject and dream?

_____

_____

_____

_____

Go back to your list of the qualities for reject girls and dream girls. First, list the qualities of the dream girl that you don't particularly admire, and explain why.

_____

_____

_____

_____

Now list the qualities of the reject girl that you like, and explain why.

_____

_____

_____

_____

_____

Think of a quality you have, but don't like. Can you find a positive way to look at it? For example, if you're shy like Natasha, what are some situations where being naturally reserved would help?

_____

_____

_____

_____

_____

...and more to do!

Write about your qualities that you don't particularly like. Can you think of the reasons why? How important are they to you? How do they affect your life? Do you think they affect other people's perception of you?

_____

_____

_____

_____

_____

_____

_____

_____

_____

_____

_____

_____

16 survey says—what pop culture is telling you

starting off ...

Pop culture is what is in the moment, what you're bombarded with when you flip through teen magazines or turn on the television, and it's hard to resist. Whenever you see the glossy ads of a rail-thin model sporting a Kate Spade handbag as the next must-have accessory for the fall season, do you have a life-sized picture of asking your mom for a $300 handbag to take on the school bus? Well, maybe you don't. Be very clear, though; pop culture is telling you to fit in by having the "right" clothes from the "right" store, wearing the "right" colors for makeup, and listening to the "right" kind of music. What you need to do is learn how to separate the literal messages from the underlying messages and make your own decisions.

For the following snippets, describe what the literal messages and the underlying messages are.

Use Dano deodorant. The next time you're really close to that special someone, you'll be sure that all he senses is the calm you.

_____

_____

_____

_____

Heavy period? Use ultra-absorbent Wedges and make sure nobody knows from your clothes what time of the month it is.

_____

_____

_____

_____

_____

Worried about dingy teeth when prom night rolls around? Always trying to cover your mouth when the school pictures are taken? Slap a Gleam Strip in, wait a minute, and what do you know? Suddenly you're the ultragleamy prom queen!

_____

_____

_____

_____

_____

Dandruff got you down in your crowd? Try Downless Dreads if your black sweater is constantly peppered with unsightly flakes.

_____

_____

_____

_____

_____

Tired of last year's boring lowrider jeans? Try Brand-O, the super-skin tight pair that's bound to make you the leader of your pack.

_____

_____

_____

_____

_____

...and more to do!

Respond to the following:

What do these snippets of advertising lingo appeal to? How could they make a person feel insecure? What values and qualities do you feel secure about in yourself? What aspects of yourself make you feel insecure? Why? What part does pop culture play in that insecurity?

_____

_____

_____

_____

_____

_____

_____

_____

_____

_____

17 you're so not that!

starting off ...

You've done it. Come on, you know you have—just admit it. You've made a snap, easy-as-pie judgment about someone based on a chance remark, or, even worse, on a shade of neon pink lip gloss. Okay, maybe this is a slight exaggeration, but if you're like most people, you're bound to have made a quick assessment based on nothing more than a casual glance.

Is there anything wrong with snap judgments? Plenty. For a start, they're often unfairly negative. Popular culture screams at us to make such judgments because, let's face it, that's what attracts readers and viewers. It's far more fascinating to read about your favorite star's battles with cellulite or alcohol than about her kindness to abandoned cats. What's more, these snap judgments can stop you from finding the essence of goodness in someone who might just be your newest great friend.

Here's an example: Gisele, the new girl in eighth grade, strode into the cafeteria. Alicia and her BFF, Maria, couldn't believe their eyes. They knew she was from a large city someplace, but why was she dressed so Goth? Everything was black, black, and blacker, from the too-thick eyeliner, to the safety pins in her stockings, to the multiple piercings in her cheeks, lips, nose, ears, and belly button. Even her hair was twisted in dreadlocks, which hung down in clumps.

Suddenly Alicia and Maria heard a commotion, and Gisele's smoker-husky voice cut through the din of the crowd. "Hey, you're both in my science class. Mind if I sit here?" As she smiled, they caught a glint of her double-pierced tongue.

Alicia and Maria just looked at each other in amazement.

What have Alicia and Maria judged Gisele by?

_____

_____

_____

Are they justified in doing so? Why or why not?

_____

_____

_____

Can you think of ways they can get to know Gisele?

_____

_____

_____

Is there anything in Gisele's manner that is unfriendly?

_____

_____

_____

How would you judge Gisele?

_____

_____

_____

Why do you think Gisele has chosen to dress this way?

_____

_____

_____

Write a paragraph that describes what happens after Gisele sits down.

_____

_____

_____

_____

_____

_____

_____

_____

_____

_____

...and more to do!

When the shoe is on the other foot, we sometimes begin to feel sympathy for those whom we've judged hastily. Write about a time where you were judged superficially. How did you feel? How did the other people react? Was their judgment of you fair? What, if any, were the repercussions of their judgment?

_____

_____

_____

_____

_____

_____

_____

_____

_____

_____

_____

_____

18 know yourself

starting off ...

Okay, now you have a sense of how unfairly we sometimes pass judgment, especially if that judgment is based on the way a person looks or speaks. So what if someone blurts out a wrong answer in English class that leaves everyone practically rolling on the floor? It doesn't mean she's a total loser. It just means she's like everyone else: occasionally wrong, sometimes funny, and always unique.

You can learn to think deeper and suspend the rush to judge. Consider what qualities and characteristics you like in a friend. Is she a good listener? Is she sympathetic when you have a problem, like when your boyfriend broke up with you in front of everyone in gym class? When you're making plans, does she insist on going to the mall (her choice) or to the movies (your choice)? Does she keep in touch with you, or does she call only when she needs a shoulder to cry on, like once a month? When someone offers a joint, is she the first one to accept, even though she doesn't do drugs? Or does she resist the pressure?

Are you beginning to see the path here? Judgment is just that: judgment. Acceptance or tolerance is based on recognizing qualities.

Using this list of words as a springboard, write a paragraph describing what popular culture tells us to look for in a friend.

Open-Minded	A Good Leader	Courageous	Civic-Minded
Studious	Ethical	Adventurous	Carefree
Creative	Honest	Empathetic	Humorous
Pretty	Popular	Exclusive	Well-Dressed

_____

_____

_____

_____

_____

_____

_____

_____

_____

_____

_____

_____

_____

...and more to do!

Now choose at least five of these qualities that you yourself look for in a friend. Explain why each quality is important to you. How many of your friends possess these qualities? Were they immediately apparent when you met these friends for the first time?

_____

_____

_____

_____

_____

_____

_____

_____

_____

_____

_____

_____

clichés, clichés, clichés

starting off ...

Trite expressions and words—the hackneyed phrases that we use to describe or to judge others—are all around us. Those worn-out expressions can be like blinders that stop us from seeing what someone is really like. When you begin to refine your expressions, you're taking the first step to identifying what's actually beneath a person's appearance.

Okay, it's back to Gisele's story. "So what's Gisele really like?" asked Heather, running to catch up with Alicia and Maria.

Maria and Alicia exchanged looks and then burst out laughing. "Ohmigod," they said simultaneously, and then burst into peals of laughter all over again.

"Does the word 'skank' mean anything to you?" asked Maria.

Heather squealed. "Skank—that's harsh."

"Either that, or else she's just totally, completely weird," said Alicia, "with her black nail polish and black lipstick."

Heather nodded, frowning. "Yeah," she said, "I see what you mean." Then she added quizzically, "But what's she really like?"

Did Maria and Alicia really describe Gisele or did they just describe her appearance?

_____

_____

_____

Why aren't Maria and Alicia able to articulate anything meaningful about Gisele?

_____

_____

_____

What's missing in their description? Why have they omitted it?

_____

_____

_____

Does Heather get a full picture of what Gisele is like? Why or why not?

_____

_____

_____

...and more to do!

Write a paragraph in which you describe your best friend's qualities, using clichés, common phrases, or words like these: awesome, cool, superbrainiac, stylin', weird, hottie, Goth.

_____

_____

_____

_____

_____

_____

Reread the paragraph. Does it present her in a true light? Why or why not? Now rewrite the paragraph using words that are fresh and original.

_____

_____

_____

_____

_____

_____

20 beauty: skin deep or inner?

starting off ...

Real beauty goes beyond what pop culture sets as the standard; it involves what is unique about someone. For example, imagine you have one friend who's short and round. She has masses of curly red hair, an infectious laugh, and energy that galvanizes the room when she walks in. Your other friend, tall, coolly elegant and poetic, barely excites a ripple. Which one is beautiful? Answer: both, although pop culture might just choose one.

Sophia and Zoe are shopping for prom dresses. Sophia, tall and dark, has broad, muscular shoulders and thighs, while Zoe, small and blonde, can scarcely wear the smallest size in the teens' department. As they're trying on one sequined gown after another, Zoe spies a turquoise halter-topped dress right at the same time Sophia does.

"It's gorgeous," breathes Zoe.

"The perfect one," agrees Sophia. "So what should we do, go to the prom as Frick and Frack?"

Just then a saleswoman bustles up to them, her sleek hair perfectly draped over one side of her face.

"Wow," she squeaks at Sophia. "With your friend's figure, she'd look so hot in that turquoise one."

Sophia feels her face redden while Zoe stares at the floor pointedly for what seems like a long minute, clutching the dress. After an awkward silence, Sophia looks at her friend and says, "Ya know, that's exactly what I was thinking. That dress would be perfect on you, girlfriend."

Just then a chocolate brown one-shouldered dress happens to catch her eye. "Say, look at this one," she says. "With my shoulders, this would look way better on me than that other one."

Zoe looks at Sophia, then lets out a long breath. "Last one to the dressing room is gonna have the fashion police after her!" And off they race.

Which one of the girls fits the mold of conventional beauty in your opinion? Why?

_____

_____

_____

_____

How does the saleswoman's unsolicited remark bring about a tiny crisis?

_____

_____

_____

_____

Do you think Sophia is being honest when she says that she likes the chocolate brown dress more?

_____

_____

_____

_____

How is Sophia's character revealed when she comes up with her solution?

_____

_____

_____

_____

Which one of the girls possesses a beautiful character and why?

_____

_____

_____

_____

...and more to do!

Write about a time when you felt you were being unfairly treated, compared to someone who had physical beauty. What happened? Were you able to demonstrate your beautiful qualities in other ways? How so?

_____

_____

_____

_____

_____

_____

_____

_____

_____

_____

_____

21 how much is too much?

starting off ...

You turn on the boob tube, and there's the latest hottie prancing on Malibu Beach with a couple of strings that pass for a bathing suit. You turn the channel to the shopping network, where an attractive saleswoman is hawking V-necked sweaters, clingy, yet in total contrast to the string swimsuit. What's the difference, other than a few inches of material? Well, girlfriend, the difference is simple. While the hottie is being deliberately provocative by baring almost everything, the shopping-network saleswoman is not; she's showing femininity.

Gina spotted Sandee, a girl from her homeroom. "What's up, Sandee?" she called.

Sandee turned and smiled at her. "Nothing much. What are you doing tonight?" she answered.

Gina walked over. "Nothing much. Same old, same old. Watch a DVD maybe, listen to some new tunes I just downloaded. Talk with Geoff on the phone. What about you?"

Sandee laughed. "If that's all that's going on for you, maybe you'd want to go out with Kevin. I had to turn him down for the dance because both Jared and David had already asked me out."

Gina giggled at the mental picture she suddenly had of the two boys arm wrestling for a dance with Sandee. "No, thanks. I don't need the leftovers. Besides, Geoff and I like to hang out. He's super nice, and we have fun just chilling."

"Suit yourself, girlfriend," Sandee said cheerfully and sauntered away.

As Gina watched her go, she couldn't help but notice Sandee's low-rise jeans and her low-cut, midriff sweater that managed to show most of her belly. "Hmm," she thought to herself, "maybe that's why she has dates galore." But then she remembered Sandee's big laugh and easy way with a joke and realized that that just might be part of the secret of her social life.

What do Sandee's clothes suggest about her? How does that match with what Gina knows of her personality?

_____

_____

_____

_____

Do you think Sandee attracts boys based on her personality? On her clothing? On both?

_____

_____

_____

_____

What pitfalls might Sandee run into when she dates?

_____

_____

_____

_____

...and more to do!

Write about a situation where one of your friends was dressed in a provocative manner and attracted attention. What was the reaction of the other girls? What was the reaction of the boys?

_____

_____

_____

_____

_____

_____

_____

_____

_____

_____

_____

You know the old saw—honesty is the best policy—or the equally moldy one—you catch more flies with honey than with vinegar. Face it, most of the time, you try to tiptoe around people's feelings, especially the girls in your clique, because you don't want a reputation as a witch. But you can learn to walk the thin line between being blatantly honest (which can be hurtful) and being nice to the point of mush.

Scenario 1

Samantha and Morgan were in the yearbook room, looking at photographs for the upcoming annual edition. As they pored over the pictures, Samantha suddenly spotted one of Morgan at the homecoming dance. Only in this photograph, Morgan's strap had slipped over her shoulder and a wisp of hair had fallen in her face. Somehow the photographer had caught her at an odd angle and her satin dress showed a pouchy tummy.

Samantha grabbed the photo out of Morgan's hand. "This can't be on the eighth-grade composite page. Ohmigod—just look at you. You're like five miles of bad road!" She turned to Morgan. "You know, you really don't photograph well at all."

Scenario 2

Samantha and Morgan were in the yearbook room, looking at photographs for the upcoming annual edition. As they pored over the pictures, Samantha suddenly spotted one of Morgan at the homecoming dance. Only in this photograph, Morgan's strap had slipped over her shoulder, and a wisp of hair had fallen in her face. Somehow the photographer had caught her at an odd angle and her satin dress showed a pouchy tummy. Samantha took the photo and said slowly, "It's all right. Your hair was a nice length. We'll see if we can fit it in somehow."

Morgan cringed inwardly and thought to herself, "Does she really think that's the best photo they have of me?"

In scenario 1, how would you describe Samantha's reaction to the photo?

_____

_____

_____

How do you think Morgan reacted to Samantha's comment? What could she have said?

_____

_____

_____

Do you think Samantha was being deliberately cruel? Why or why not?

_____

_____

_____

How can being too blunt in this instance be unsettling for Morgan?

_____

_____

_____

In scenario 2, why didn't Samantha tell Morgan the truth about what she thought of the photo?

_____

_____

_____

What does Samantha need to say, in your opinion?

_____

_____

_____

How can Samantha's not telling the truth hurt in scenario 2? What emotions does it cause for Morgan?

_____

_____

_____

...and more to do!

Now rewrite the scenario and have Samantha honestly but politely decline the picture for the yearbook.

_____

_____

_____

_____

_____

_____

_____

_____

_____

_____

_____

_____

independent vs. submissive

23

starting off ...

Have you ever been in the situation where your clique was insisting on a course of action that you just weren't comfortable with? What was your response? Were you quiet, nodding politely? Or were you up front about what you felt? Wanting to agree and go along with the group is natural because, let's face it, sometimes you just don't want to rock the boat. But in this activity, you'll find out when it's all right to rock the boat because it means standing up for what you believe in.

Jasmine and her friends were hanging out at the mall, like they did every Saturday night, because it was a place to meet up with the boys from their school.

Suddenly Alexis said to the others, "Let's go buy some CDs. I know there are a couple of new releases."

So off they trooped to the store. They had to pass through the security barrier as usual, and then they all went to the various listening stations, under the watchful eye of the store clerk.

After a while, Alexis whispered to Jasmine, "I'm so tired of that jerk giving us the evil eye. Who does he think he is? Just because we're thirteen, we're all juvenile delinquents?"

Jasmine whispered back, "I know what you mean. He's so annoying."

Alexis said suddenly, "Let's give him something to really get mad about! You know, if we load up our pockets with tons of coins, we'll set off the security detectors, and when he searches us, he'll be mad that we're clean!"

Jasmine felt uneasy. Yeah, it wasn't stealing, which she knew she wouldn't do, but it was razzing the guy who, after all, was only doing his job. Still, Alexis was the unofficial leader of the clique. Jasmine said hesitantly, "Well, okay, I guess."

Alexis called over the other girls, and they surreptitiously poured their change into her and Jasmine's pockets when the store clerk was looking elsewhere. Then Alexis led the way out of the store and through the security gates with Jasmine meekly following.

The alarms pierced the air. Lights started to flash. The clerk came running over to where the girls had stopped dead in their tracks. "Hold it right there, ladies," he said gruffly. "Just want to make sure that a CD didn't make its way out with you."

Jasmine felt her face flush. Why had she gone along just to be nice?

Meanwhile, Alexis was being her usual defiant, sassy self. "We didn't do anything. Why are you picking on us? See, I don't have anything in my pockets!" With that she turned the lining of her pocket inside out, and a pound of quarters and dimes rolled out onto the floor.

The clerk turned to Jasmine. "What about you?"

Jasmine opened her pocket wide. Nothing but a bunch of silver coins lay nestled in the lining.

The clerk scowled at both of them. "This is your idea of a joke," he sputtered. "Some joke. Let me have your names and addresses." They gave them to him meekly. Then he said, "Now get out of here and don't come back again!" He turned on his heels, and all the girls left, laughing and chatting among themselves.

Inside, though, Jasmine was feeling uneasy. Why had she done this? Was it really wrong?

Why was Jasmine reluctant to go along with Alexis's idea?

_____

_____

_____

What is your opinion of Alexis's idea? Was it wrong of her to want Jasmine to go along with it? What does it indicate about her character?

_____

_____

_____

Why does Jasmine go along with the idea?

_____

_____

_____

How could Jasmine have handled the situation with Alexis and still kept her standing in the group?

_____

_____

_____

Was there really any harm done with Alexis's so-called joke? What were the long-term consequences? Was the joke worth the consequences? Why or why not?

_____

_____

_____

...and more to do!

Now write an alternate version of the story in which Jasmine chooses an independent course of action and decides that she's not going to go along with Alexis's idea.

_____

_____

_____

_____

_____

_____

_____

_____

_____

_____

_____

_____

part 3

*

to clique or not to clique

Face it, we're all part of cliques, whether we want to call them that or not. But have you ever thought that you knew everyone in your clique, only to make a chance remark at BFF's locker, and then have no one talking to you the next day? Suddenly a week later, the freeze has melted and you're back in everyone's good graces. Hey, what happened, you fume silently to yourself. What happened, girlfriend, is the power of the clique.

In this section, you'll find out about creating expectations and guidelines for how you and your friends want to be friends. Remember those history lessons from school? Well, even cliques need rules, and rules are best made when everyone has a say in them. It's democracy in action.

24 who makes your clique click?

starting off ...

In most groups, people play certain roles. Just look at your own family. Who's the responsible one, the clown, the goody two-shoes? The same is true for your clique, including you. Are you the one who's always in charge of making the social arrangements, such as IM-ing all the buds on the list about which movie to go to and what time to meet? Who's always the one to remember birthdays? Who can be counted on to be satisfied and who to complain?

It was a typical day at Lincoln Middle School. Nicole spied Danielle and the gang at their usual table in the lunchroom and rushed over with her tray of fries and chili dogs. "Hi there! What's up?" she asked.

Nita said, "Nothing. Just trying to lose ten pounds while we wait for Jen to come so we can talk about the homecoming dance."

Jen suddenly appeared. "Did I hear the word 'dance'? Okay, here's the deal. We'll meet at the coffee shop at eight and go pick up Michaela and Allie."

Nita, sitting in the corner and toying with her salad, piped up. "You mean we have to walk? God, I'm gonna break out in a sweat and I already use an industrial-strength deodorant!"

The girls giggled.

Lily said, "What about me, guys? I wanna come. Can I come too?"

"Sure," said Danielle absently. "Don't keep us waiting, Lily. I'm meeting Dylan at the dance."

Jen added, "Just be ready and waiting at seven, Lily."

"Jeez, guys," whispered Nicole as two boys strutted by their table. "Did you know that Eric and Connor are going alone to the dance? I just heard in fifth period that Connor broke up by text with the newbie. Can you believe that?"

Draw a line that matches each girl with the role she plays in the clique:

Danielle   Organizer and secretary

Nicole   Hanger-on

Nita   Gossip girl

Jen   Head honcho, a.k.a. she who must be obeyed

Lily   Clown

...and more to do!

Now it's time to pare down to the essentials. How do the members of your clique act within each of these roles? Can you give examples?

_____

_____

_____

_____

_____

_____

What is your own role within the clique? Is it a role you play in other group situations? Do you enjoy it? Why or why not? If you don't enjoy it, what can you do to change it?

_____

_____

_____

_____

_____

_____

_____

starting off ...

Stuff happens. All of a sudden, just when you and your BFFs are getting along famously, suddenly—bam!—a look, a pointed remark, and it's as though World War III has broken out. What happened to cause this emotional bomb? Who is responsible, or is it just the ebb and flow of cliquedom in operation?

It's Taco Day at school, and you and your friends are chowing down on the only decent lunch the cafeteria ever serves. Suddenly Marcy leans closer to you and says, "Did you know that Annie broke up with Michael yesterday? Now she's going out with his best friend Isaiah!" At that exact moment, both you and Marcy turn to look at Annie, who's holding forth at the other end of the table, like the head honcho you all know her to be.

Annie's voice cuts like a knife across all the chitchat. "What are you two whispering about?" she demands.

Silence. You can hear a pin drop. Marcy turns and faces Annie, then delivers a diversionary bomb. "Nothing, Annie, nothing important anyway." Then Marcy gives you an obvious wink and turns to the girl on her other side to repeat the news.

Marcy is playing telephone as a basis for a power play, and you can probably imagine what happens next.

Describe a similar situation in the clique you belong to—a time when someone stepped out of her role to challenge the head honcho, either directly or indirectly. What were the results? What was the fallout among the various members of the clique and why?

_____

_____

_____

_____

_____

_____

_____

_____

_____

_____

_____

_____

...and more to do!

Now write about your own experience. Have you ever challenged the head honcho directly, or have you been like Marcy, the telephone girl? How did that feel to you? Have you challenged other members of the clique? Why? What was the fallout?

_____

_____

_____

_____

_____

_____

_____

_____

_____

_____

_____

_____

26 the enemy is across the room, and they're looking at you

starting off ...

You know who they are—the enemy. Hey, they all might be really pretty or speak with sweet, girly-girl voices, but it doesn't change who they are—the enemy. They might be a rival clique who figure out all the rules and then try to impose them on everyone. Or they could be the so-called anticlique, bound together by their hatred of the leading clique. Whoever and whatever the cliques are defined to be in your school, you, girlfriend, need to analyze who they are and what they appear to stand for.

Amanda and Amber belong to the anti-cheerleading clique at school. The members of their clique are loud, sassy, and fun loving. And they also just happen to excel on all the sports teams.

The cheerleading clique—anti-sporty, pro-girly, and in general stuck-up—apparently reigns supreme in the corridors of the school but not on the playing fields, except for cheering the boys from the sidelines.

Amanda gets a text message from Amber, who says that Cindy, one of the cheesy cheerleaders, has just dissed a member of their own clique. "I heard her call Carly a muffin top with no butt!" texts Amber. "Who are they to call her a muffin top!"

Amanda texts back, "Really?"

"Yes. This means action," texts Amber.

If you were to write the rest of this scene, what would Amanda and Amber do next?

_____

_____

_____

_____

_____

Do you think getting revenge is the solution to the rivalry that exists between the two cliques? Why or why not?

_____

_____

_____

_____

_____

_____

_____

_____

_____

_____

...and more to do!

Draw a diagram that names the various cliques at your school and where they hang out.

How do you think your clique reacts when someone disses them?

_____

_____

_____

_____

What do you believe your clique's values are?

_____

_____

_____

Describe an incident between your clique and a rival clique where your group showed their values. How did you feel about being a member of your clique?

_____

_____

_____

_____

_____

_____

27 rules, rules, rules

starting off ...

You know about rules, right? Your parents, wise people that they are (maybe an exaggeration, but you get the point) understandably have a ton of them for you. And undoubtedly they're all designed to help you, streamline your life, instill discipline, and develop a sense of responsibility within you, and so on—aaargh! In fact, if you follow the logical progression, isn't this why you can't spend the entire weekend shopping at the mall or go out on the night before a big test? But while your parents might have obvious, concrete rules, the rules of cliques are usually a bit more subtle, so much so that you may not be really conscious of them.

You can examine the subtleties of your clique and figure out what the rules are. Think of the obvious rules and place them in the column headed Right Out There. Scratch your head a little more, and put the less obvious ones in the Beneath the Surface list. There's an example to get you started.

Right out There	Beneath the Surface
Be polite to adults.	Make fun of them behind their backs.

Now's it's time to figure out what kind of code your clique is living by. Examine each rule in both columns and put a check mark next to the ones you think have redeeming value. To help you decide, ask yourself who benefits from it, and how. If a rule doesn't seem to have value, decide why.

...and more to do!

Write about a time when you, girlfriend, actually disagreed with one of these rules. What happened? How did the other members of the clique react? What was the outcome?

_____

_____

_____

_____

_____

_____

_____

_____

_____

_____

_____

starting off ...

What if one day you could wave a magic wand over your friends and change their behavior? No, you say, you wouldn't change anything, not even a teensy-weensy little thing, not even the way your BFF sometimes ignores you when she starts to flirt with the quarterback on the football team? Let's face it—you're not perfect and neither are they. But sometimes you might just wish that a tiny aspect of your group friendship would change. It could be how you treat each other on a daily basis or what you dish about or the rules that you all abide by, spoken or unspoken.

Imagine that it's a new day at school and for some weird, inexplicable reason, you're now Queen of the Universe. You have the power and the authority to decide what new rules are going to be instituted and what old ones are going to be ditched.

So your first act is to decree that all your friends need to stop chewing wads of bubblegum when they chat on the phone. Or wait, maybe you'll decide that you all have to call each other by cloying endearments, such as "Hey buttercup, whatup?" Maybe you won't allow them to talk to the cool guys in school unless you get to talk to them first.

No, just kidding. In a dream world, no one as the head honcho of a clique would have that kind of authority. Or would they? Think about it.

Take the rules you listed and evaluated in the last activity and rewrite them so that they are more positive. For example:

Everyone in your clique is always invited to a member's party would become Everyone also invites one member from another clique to a party. See where this is going?

_____

_____

_____

_____

_____

_____

_____

_____

_____

_____

_____

Now reread the rules. What kind of pictures come into your mind about this newly created code of rules?

_____

_____

_____

_____

_____

_____

_____

_____

...and more to do!

Write a scene where you and your friends are living by the new, slightly improved rules. What are the positive results of the new rules? What are the negative results?

_____

_____

_____

_____

_____

_____

_____

_____

_____

_____

_____

_____

starting off ...

When friends bond, it's based on solid reasons. Maybe you find the same movies funny or you play the same sport or you like the same music group, the Flying Death Bunnies. Okay, just kidding about the bunnies. But whatever it is, something brings you and your group of friends together. There are also things that might tear you apart, like gossip and bullying. Or maybe it's ganging up on someone, even in your own clique, one of the fringe element who hangs around the periphery. Or maybe it's a matter of someone, no names here, who is being just way too judgmental.

Just like the good old U.S. of A. has the Declaration of Independence and the Bill of Rights, you're going to write an honest-to-goodness bill of rights for your clique.

First, start with a belief paragraph. What are your values and ethics as a group? Remember, this doesn't mean that you always act in this way, but it's what you strive for.

Then in the second paragraph, include a slogan that expresses the ideas in the belief paragraph. Try to make it snappy.

Then in the final paragraph, list your slightly improved and positive rules outlined in Activity 28.

activity 29 ✳ girlfriends' bill of rights

...and more to do!

What are the values that belong to only you? What are the values that belong to the clique? In what ways do they differ?

_____

_____

_____

Which values seem to be better for the group? Why?

_____

_____

_____

Write a scenario in which you pitch your bill of rights to your clique. Be sure to include their reactions.

_____

_____

_____

_____

_____

_____

_____

30 analyze this—the cliques at your school

starting off ...

We all have stereotypes that somehow pop into our heads when we least expect them. You definitely know what that's like when you see a girl in Goth garb. All of a sudden, your stereotyping meter starts whirring away and making assumptions. But as you've already found out, what you see is not always what you get. Take cliques, for example. Earlier in this book, you practiced your artistic skills and drew a map of where all the cliques usually hung out in your school. In fact, you labeled them. How did you come by those labels, girlfriend? Let's be totally, totally honest. Was it stereotypical thinking?

Now, for some fun, try to use positive words to describe what your clique does. But remember that even positive words can reflect stereotyped thinking. Fill in the blanks to find out.

When my _____ clique gets together at lunch
                             (adjective)

time, we always _____ . Then when we're finished,
                    (verb)

_____walks over to
                  (name of a clique role)

_____ and says
                  (name of a clique role)

_____ . Then we leave
           (your choice here)

_____.
        (adverb)

In _____ class, we try
(adjective + subject name)

to sit together. When we can't, we sit behind _____.
(adjective + noun)

Then we usually _____ during the entire class.
(verb + object)

After school, we stay connected by _____. And if we decide
(verb ending in -ing)

we want to _____, we _____
(verb)   (verb)

our parents by phone. They're not _____.
(adjective)

...and more to do!

Now try to look at your clique through someone else's eyes. Yeah, this is tough, but try really hard to avoid those noxious stereotypes.

Pretend you're the teacher of the class above. Write a paragraph describing how you, the teacher, perceive this clique. To add to this lovely pudding mix, you're going to recommend a group to be selected for a special field trip to Mexico or Paris. Would this clique be selected? Why or why not?

_____

_____

_____

_____

_____

_____

_____

Now pretend you are the head honcho of the rival clique. Write a paragraph about how the teacher of the class perceives your clique and its various members. Remember, this rival clique is also being considered for this fabulous trip. As head honcho extraordinaire, write about the values and qualities that your group possesses compared to the other clique.

_____

_____

_____

_____

_____

In a third paragraph, pretend that you're the principal of your school. The teacher has come to see you, asking for help to decide which clique gets to go to Mexico or Paris or Las Vegas (just kidding about Las Vegas). Write a dialogue in which you discuss the two cliques and the reasons why one should go and the other should not.

_____

_____

_____

_____

_____

part 4

*

cyber stalker 101

It's a night like any other. You know, the usual: dinner, dishes, and then homework before you can watch your favorite TV show. There you are on your computer, doing your math homework and IM-ing the people in your clique, when suddenly the screen name of one of your friends pops up. She then proceeds to tell you and your IM buddies that you're a skank, that you've never seen a deodorant stick, and that you cheated on a math test—all this from a girl that you went to the mall with last Saturday. And the written missiles just keep coming until you sign off.

Whether it's a post on MySpace, a flaming e-mail, or an IM that gets people from your buddy list chatting, don't make the mistake of dashing off a response when you're mad. Think about how to get the result that you want. After all, you're entitled to be online without being dissed by nasty people.

31 know thyself—are you a cyberbully?

Circle the answers to these questions.

Have you ever used someone else's identity in a chat room or in an IM message?   Yes   No

Have you ever shared an embarrassing secret about someone else online?   Yes   No

Have you ever sent or posted a gross image of someone online or by cell-phone camera?   Yes   No

Have you ever used profanity or angry language with someone online or by text?   Yes   No

Have you ever bombarded someone with nasty e-mails, IMs, or texts?   Yes   No

'Fess up; if you've answered yes to even one of these questions, you've crossed the line. Girlfriend, you've been a cyberbully.

Oh no, you protest, not me. Besides, it was totally a joke, and no one's feelings got seriously hurt. But the truth remains—it is cyberbullying, regardless of intention. Think of it this way: When you're in cyberspace, no one can see your expression or hear your tone of voice, the clues that let others understand your intent. All they see are the words or the image.

...and more to do!

For each question that you answered yes to, write about one time when you cyberbullied. Were there any consequences? How did you feel? How do you think the other person felt?

_____

_____

_____

_____

_____

_____

_____

_____

_____

_____

_____

_____

_____

_____

_____

_____

_____

_____

Let's say that someone has taken a picture of you rooting around in your nose in the library just when you thought nobody was looking. All of a sudden, it's being sent to everyone's cell phones with a text message that proclaims, "Looks like she's hungry for lunch!" Describe your feelings and your actions.

_____

_____

_____

_____

_____

_____

_____

_____

starting off ...

Some people out there in cyberspace take a particularly vicious delight in ruining the reps of others or, at the very least, making someone's life a living nightmare. It may begin innocently enough with a couple of online impersonations, and then just as rapidly, it escalates into vitriol. And guess what? You might be the target.

Read this texting to see if you can identify exactly when and how the cyberbully starts to get out of line.

You: R u there?

Bully: What's up?

You: Nothing—saw you talking with a cute guy

Bully: What—him? Jealous? LOL—EG

You: Just curious

Bully: None of your freakin business. SSIF

You: Give it a rest

Bully: SIS!

At what point in this texting does the friend (major air quotes here!) become a bully? When does the tone of the text start to change?

_____

_____

_____

_____

_____

...and more to do!

Write an exchange that shows how you would you respond to the bully.

_____

_____

_____

_____

_____

_____

What do you think the bully wants from you?

_____

_____

_____

Do you think your response to the text bully would be effective? Why or why not?

_____

_____

_____

_____

_____

What would be the next step if this person keeps texting you?

_____

_____

_____

_____

_____

_____

how to defend yourself online

starting off ...

It's a big, dark, scary world out there in cyberspace. Just imagine that you're innocently sitting at your computer, chatting away, when suddenly someone slams you in an IM. Where you might have the answers in the text-messaging world (yep, you can always turn off your cell phone), IM-ing is just so ... public. Yes, you could turn off the computer, but by now everyone has seen the flame, the mock, or the jeer.

Scenario 1

Late one night, Dannie was totally bored. Bored with her little sister and bored with her parents, she decided to go online to a chat room she had found out about when she signed up for her IM service.

When she signed in, she was surprised to find an old boyfriend already there, a guy who had repeatedly asked her for dates. She shuddered when she remembered how she had said no, nicely at first, and then more emphatically when he started coming on to her in the hallway.

"So you again, skank?" he typed. "Have you tried to lead other people on, like you did with me?"

At first, Dannie ignored his taunts. But they became more vicious, until finally he typed, "For a good time, call Dannie. She's up for anything." And he even put in her number!

She was aghast. Sure, they knew each other at school, but she didn't know the rest of these people online at all. Now here was her personal cell phone number for all to see. Worst of all, he had totally ruined her reputation with his innuendo.

Scenario 2

Her homework was done and she had finished getting ready for bed when Madison decided that she would check her e-mail one last time before calling it a night. When she logged on, she noticed an interesting subject line for one of the e-mails in her in-box. It read "Two People Have a Crush on You." Intrigued, she opened it. To her horror, she saw two vulgar pictures of guys with lewd captions underneath. The e-mail said only, "You're my not-so-secret crush, baby." Then she glanced at the cc: field and found out that her entire grade had been copied on the e-mail. How could she go into school tomorrow? People might think she was the kind of girl who would think this was funny, or worse yet, had invited it! Everyone would already have seen it, and there wasn't any easy way to find out who had sent it.

Of these two scenarios, which one was more damaging? Why?

_____

_____

_____

_____

How do you suppose Madison could have avoided this kind of e-mail being sent to her?

_____

_____

_____

_____

How can Madison do damage control the next day at school? Do you think the prankster is someone in her class? What kind of gratification would that person get from her public reaction?

_____

_____

_____

_____

For Dannie, the problem is a bit stickier. How would you suggest that she handle it with the spurned boy at her school?

_____

_____

_____

How should Dannie handle the incident in general? Why?

_____

_____

_____

...and more to do!

Write about a time that you were harassed either in a chat room, an IM, or an e-mail. What did you do? What did you feel like? How did you react? Did you tell your parents or teacher? What was the final result?

_____

_____

_____

_____

_____

_____

_____

_____

_____

_____

_____

_____

starting off …

So what if the world is a dark and scary place? At least your friends are warm and funny. But are they always? Keep in mind that everyone is capable of being a cyberbully given the opportunity, and your friends are no exception. Remember the cardinal rule of cybercommunication: humor and teasing do not translate well. Save it for face to face, and keep it light online. As for retaliation, forget it. It doesn't work and it just keeps the problem escalating.

Scenario 1

Rosanna logged on to her IM service and saw two of her buddies chitchatting away about what they were going to wear to school for Picture Day.

"Red top with the gold dangle earrings?" Rocgirl234 asked.

"Go with green—better for your complexion," responded TrueBlue526.

To Rosanna's surprise, she saw her screen name, Rosieatt, come on. "Give it up, you two wide loads. The camera is definitely going to add ten pounds to your chipmunk-cheek faces."

Rocgirl234 shot back: "Who made you Lord Ruler of the Universe? Last time I checked, you weren't exactly a Tyra Banks!"

TrueBlue526 chimed in. "You are totally over the top, moron!"

Rosanna quickly typed: "That wasn't me, seriously, guys."

But by this time, the two girls had logged off in a huff, leaving the fake Rosanna hee-heeing. "Know who this is?" she warbled, if one can warble online. "It's Amy."

"Amy, how could you! Call them and tell them that it was you!" Rosanna typed.

There was no response, and then Amy logged off.

Scenario 2

Esperanza logged on to MySpace one night when she wanted to catch a break between her algebra and social studies homework. She thought she had done a cute job of posting pictures of her BFFs at her last birthday party, especially the catchy captions.

To her horror, she saw that someone had posted comments about every single photograph, ranging from "She thinks she's so freakin' cool" to "Even Britney Spears wouldn't be caught dead in this outfit!"

Then she looked farther down and saw that her BFFs had started posting outraged responses to the comments. Suddenly, her cell phone began to ring, and Rebecca, her best friend of all time, shouted at her, "It's not funny! Clean it up right now before the whole school knows!"

And just while Rebecca was reaming her out, Esperanza got a call-waiting beep.

It was Josie, giggling. "Did I get you good or did I get you good?"

Esperanza felt her anger boil up. She swallowed hard before she started to respond.

How can Rosanna make sure that no one hijacks her identity again?

_____

_____

_____

At what point did Amy cross the line into unacceptable teasing? What was the reaction of Rosanna and her friends?

_____

_____

_____

How should Rosanna deal with Amy? And should it be privately or publicly?

_____

_____

_____

If you were Esperanza, how would you respond to Josie?

_____

_____

_____

How can Esperanza make sure that none of her friends, including the infamous Josie, ever post insulting remarks on her profile page?

_____

_____

_____

If you were part of Esperanza's clique, how would you make cyberteasing among your friends a thing of the past?

_____

_____

_____

What agreements, if any, do you and your friends have about hijacking each other's identities online?

_____

_____

_____

At what point should Esperanza and Rosanna involve their parents?

_____

_____

_____

...and more to do!

Write a dialogue between Rosanna and Amy when they see each other the next day in school. How does Rosanna handle Amy's cyberteasing? What is Amy's reaction?

_____

_____

_____

_____

_____

_____

_____

_____

_____

_____

_____

35 how's your cyber IQ?

> ## starting off ...
>
> How can you avoid being the bull's-eye target of a cyberbully? And how can you dodge becoming one yourself? Well, part of the answer is being cybersmart: knowing how to behave when you can't see other people's facial expressions and how to keep yourself safe online. Why should cyberspace be any different from real life? Would you snarl at your BFF, "Who died and left you in charge?" when she says she wants to see the latest sci-fi movie and you want to see a chick flick? Then why would you text her "wdalyic"?

Answer the following multiple-choice questions to find out how cybersmart you are.

1. When you write e-mails, text messages, or IMs, you

    A. Think nothing of using all caps to get your points across

    B. Use grammatically constructed sentences

    C. Use short, concise phrases

2. When you get a particularly good deal in your e-mail box, you

    A. Read it through for information

    B. Send it to the trash immediately (after all, it may contain a virus or just be a plain old hoax)

    C. Forward it to everyone you know (hey, a bargain is a bargain)

3. When you communicate with your buds through e-mail, you

    A. Copy all of them (dish is to be shared, right?)

    B. Guard their privacy and their e-mail addresses by bcc-ing them

    C. Pick and choose whom you're going to e-mail

4. When you im or e-mail friends, you

   A. Use a lot of multiple exclamation points and question marks

   B. Try to be as clear as possible

   C. Use text message abbreviations (who has time to write?)

5. When someone tells you about a really good chat room where you can meet cool people online, you

   A. Read through the information on the website

   B. Check the chat to see if the atmosphere is friendly and the chat is about subjects you're interested in

   C. Immediately dive right in and sign up

6. When you sign up for MySpace or an IM service, you

   A. Really just want to set up a page and restrict it to your circle of friends

   B. Just love to fill out the detailed profile information so that you can have a really, really big network of friends

   C. Avoid giving out any personal information

7. Whenever you're logged on in a chat room or IM and you're totally bored with the discussion, you

   A. Sign off

   B. Post bogus things

   C. Say good-bye and then sign off

8. When you post on your bff's myspace page, you

   A. Try to be funny at any cost

   B. Use sarcastic, teasing humor to tweak her

   C. Make sure your funny remarks are also kind

9. When you get an e-mail from a friend who's passed on a juicy rumor from the Internet, you

    A. Forward it, along with other outrageous online rumors

    B. Read through it carefully and delete it (after all, it seems like spam to you)

    C. Check the truthfulness of the rumor by going to such websites as Snopes.com.

Answers

1. C is the best answer, although be mindful that B is important too. Cyberspace is the kind of writing tablet that demands short, concise phrases at least in the e-mails and texts you're sending to your friends. To people you don't know, use grammatically correct sentences. And above all, never use screaming caps. It's LIKE SHOUTING. See—doesn't that sound really loud?

2. B is the best answer. Most of the deals that come through e-mail are just too good to be true; they are also a way to get you to give marketers personal information.

3. B and C are both pretty good. You never know where an e-mail might be forwarded, so if there's information that you want everyone in your clique to have, then use the blind copy field. C is also correct because some communication is best kept private.

4. B is the best one. Abbreviations are fine as long as you're sure everyone knows them, but the main thing is clarity. Avoid the exclamation points and question marks because often they come off as sarcasm. And remember, you are responsible for maintaining your relationships.

5. A and B are both good. Before you jump right in, you might even want to consult with your parents. Then do a little investigation by reading the chat room's FAQ section. Find out if the chat room's discussion is monitored and if the subjects they talk about are interesting to you.

6. Both A and C are good. It really depends what you want from posting a profile. Some people want to keep in touch with a network, and other want to restrict it. Try for a balance if you can—just don't provide lots of personal information.

7. C is best. Netiquette demands politeness, and people just might want to know if you're leaving for a minute or for the night.

8. C is best. After all, just think about how you, yes you, want to be treated. Doesn't teasing get really tiresome, after all?

9. B and C are both right. It does depend on how much information you like to send around to your friends. But hey, if you're going to send information, try to verify it. Don't accept everything that you read on the Net at face value.

...and more to do!

Pretend you've gotten a really rude text from one of your BFFs. Using all your cybersmarts, how do you respond?

_____

_____

_____

_____

_____

_____

Now imagine that you're going to post something on a friend's MySpace profile page. You want to strike a balance between being witty and being sincere. What do you write?

_____

_____

_____

_____

_____

_____

writing a profile bound for trouble 36

---

starting off ...

Okay, you've talked about it with your parents, and they've allowed you to post a profile on MySpace. Yeah, they've warned you about all the usual stuff—no personal information ever, keep your language appropriate (parent translation: no profanity, no obscenities). Oh, and did they also mention that sometimes future employers check out these websites for information?

Isabella was so excited to finally, finally have her parents' permission to post a profile online. When she started her profile, she thought she would go for a really cool effect, with lots of photographs, snappy captions … you get the picture. She included her name, age, school, height, weight, and religion, and continued with: this

List of Friends: **Everyone here on this website**

Looking For: **Connections and really cute guys**

Favorite Things to Do: **Hang out in cyberspace, hang with my friends at the Wyoming Mall on Saturday night, read Harry Potter books, and listen to the Black Eyed Peas.**

Think about Isabella's profile and answer these questions.

Why might posting her religion be a problem of privacy?

_____

_____

_____

Should she restrict people's access to her profile? Why or why not?

_____

_____

_____

Where has Isabella put information that is too specific? What could someone do with this information, especially coupled with photographs of her?

_____

_____

_____

Do you think she should have put her school and her age on the profile? Why or why not?

_____

_____

_____

...and more to do!

Rewrite Isabella's profile to make it safer for viewing by the world at large.

_____

_____

_____

_____

Now write a profile Isabella could use if she decides to make it available only to her circle of friends.

_____

_____

_____

_____

Reread both profiles. Which one would be the kind of profile you would be most likely to post? Why?

_____

_____

_____

_____

37 create your own sassy profile

starting off ...

Now it's your turn to write your own customized profile. Think about the image you want to project. Do you want to be thought of as strong, confident, and smart? Or do you want to be thought of as shy, insecure, and pathetic? Remember, the words you choose project an image that you'll have to live with. Be careful about using words that tantalize and tease, or when you see people face-to-face, they just might be reacting to a so-called you that doesn't even exist.

Tell whether you think each statement is true or false, and why.

1. It's okay to post as many revealing photographs as you can get away with.

_____

_____

2. You can be sarcastic when you mention other people by name.

_____

_____

3. It's totally okay to fudge the truth a bit. After all, who really cares?

_____

_____

4. Don't use abbreviations; website netiquette is a bit more formal than texting.

_____

_____

5. Never use humor in your profile; it's better to be serious at all times.

_____

_____

6. Don't bother to check your spelling or punctuation; kids are logging on to check you out, not to evaluate your English skills.

_____

_____

7. It's always cool to diss the school you're attending.

_____

_____

8. Never put down anyone else in your profile, no matter how tempting it is. Negativity attracts negativity.

_____

_____

Answers

1. False. Your image is part of your privacy, so make sure to safeguard it. Anyway, if you put a photo out there, you risk someone adding facial hair to it!

2. False. Other people are entitled to their privacy, and your sarcasm may hurt someone.

3. Well, it depends on what you mean by "a bit." Lying isn't good, but if it's so obvious you're exaggerating, go with it. For instance, if you barely top four-eleven in your espadrilles, saying you're six foot two and eighty years old might be comic exaggeration, so over the top that it's funny.

4. True. People might think you're missing part of your ability to communicate clearly.

5. False. Come on, humor is the leavening in life. Yuk it up.

6. False. Do check this stuff; you're presenting yourself without speaking, and if everything you've written is misspelled, that might affect others' impression of you.

7. Falsish. Be careful here. Naming your school would be giving away personal information. Also, some schools have policies about how much you can say. And remember, don't mention names. Other people's reps are on the line.

8. True. When you criticize others, you're saying more about yourself than about anyone else.

...and more to do!

Ready? Now that you're primed, write your own profile using the following categories: name, address, age, interests, description of your personality, and likes.

_____

_____

_____

_____

_____

_____

_____

_____

_____

_____

_____

_____

_____

_____

38 the vocabulary of texting

starting off ...

Okay, ready for a quiz? Let's see how good you are at a language that your parents probably don't understand. Just remember to save this for instant messaging and texting. Teachers and parents tend to like whole sentences.

Match the words on the following page to their definitions. Have fun and play it fair.

1. BRT   Great

2. CU   Fouled up beyond all recognition

3. EOM   See you, sweetie

4. FUBAR   In over my head

5. EG   Same place, same time

6. GR8   Just wondering

7. GTG   Snickering in silence

8. SPST   Got to go

9. TCOY   Laugh out loud

10. ILU   So stupid it's funny

11. IMU   See you

12. SYS   Thanks

13. THX   I love you

14. LOL   End of message

15. JW   Take care of yourself

16. IOMH   Evil grin

17. SSIF   I miss you

18. SIS   Be right there

Answers

1. Be right there

2. See you

3. End of message

4. Fouled up beyond all recognition

5. Evil grin

6. Great

7. Got to go

8. Same place, same time

9. Take care of yourself

10. I love you

11. I miss you

12. See you, sweetie

13. Thanks

14. Laugh out loud

15. Just wondering

16. In over my head

17. So stupid it's funny

18. Snickering in silence

...and more to do!

Ready for some kicks and giggles? Write a text message to your BFF asking for details of her breakup with her boyfriend. Remember to watch your tone.

_____

_____

_____

_____

Once you're done, reread it. Is texting suitable for heart-rending messages or expressions of sympathy? Why or why not?

_____

_____

_____

_____

_____

_____

Now write a text to your totally cool, techno-savvy dad asking him for permission to stay out later at the mall tonight.

_____

_____

_____

_____

_____

Once you're done, reread it. How does a straightforward text request compare to an emotional message?

_____

_____

_____

_____

_____

_____

starting off ...

You probably have a friend whom you can't tell secrets to; it's an unwritten guarantee that what you say will be all over everyone's IMs the next day. Think of cyberspace as like that friend: it can't keep secrets. Multiply the number of big-mouth people you know by a bazillion, and there you have the Internet—an instant recipe for privacy invasion.

Are these statements good ideas or terrible ideas? Explain the reason for your answer.

1. When I log on in a chat room, I give out my password to others if they seem trustworthy enough and if they're on my Internet service.

_____

_____

2. I fill out any online forms for something free. After all, who can turn down a really good deal?

_____

_____

3. When someone approaches me online and wants to arrange an in-person meeting, I'm sure to tell my parents first.

_____

_____

4. When I get spam in my e-mail, I just delete it. If spam continues to annoy me, I report it to the server administrator.

_____

_____

5. When I want to share a secret with a friend, I do it in person.

_____

_____

Answers

1. Terrible, really terrible idea. You're leaving yourself open to identity theft. And who cares if others use the same Internet service? It's kind of like trusting strangers just because they live in your neighborhood.

2. Nope, nope, terrible idea. Although the information might not be particularly personal, it gives the lurkers enough info on you so that they can search for you online.

3. Good idea. Your parental units will probably be a little horrified that you've met someone online, and they will have to check the person out first, even if you whine and plead and promise that you'll meet in a public place.

4. Good idea. When marketers send you spam, there are always a few unscrupulous guys who want to entice you to visit a porn site. The next thing you know, you've got e-mails in your inbox advertising breast enhancements. Many servers have an option where you can forward the e-mail and report it as spam.

5. Brilliant idea! Just be sure the friend is one you can trust.

...and more to do!

Now write a pledge that includes the specific steps you are going to take to safeguard your privacy.

_____

_____

_____

_____

_____

_____

_____

_____

_____

_____

_____

_____

40 when to activate the parental units

starting off ...

Okay, life is scary because you're being bullied online. Every day you're getting bizarro text messages, and at night your IM chats with your friends are being invaded by an ever-changing cast of screen names. You've even taken the huge, mature step of withdrawing your profile from online, but the abuse continues. What do you do? Well, call in the big guns, a.k.a. your parents. But how do you tell them?

Read these different approaches and decide which one would be the best to use with your parents.

1. Mom and Dad, can you please, please read this posting on my profile? Can you believe what Josh is saying about me? How can I possibly face him in science class tomorrow? He'll just sit there and smirk at me and then whisper something to his buddies.

2. Mom and Dad, can you help me with something right now, even before you take off your coats? I need you to read this post right away. Josh is calling me a skank, and I've gotta figure out what I need to do to get revenge.

3. Mom and Dad, why don't you both just sit down? You need a cup of coffee? Let me pour you some. Why am I acting this way? No, I don't need money to go shopping. No, it's not a boy. Du-uh, no, I'm not in trouble. Well, not the trouble you're thinking of. Forget it, I'm going upstairs until you both calm down.

4. Mom, Dad? I've got a bit of a problem online and I need your advice on how to handle it. I already removed my profile, but the problem is coming on my IMs as well as my texts.

If you've answered 4, you are so right on the mark—no drama, no let's sit-down-immediately demands, no sweet-talking to prime their anxiety.

...and more to do!

Now let's get your creativity flowing. You're the expert on your own parents. Write a dialogue in which you ask them for help. Be sure to include what you think they would suggest, based on their own skills in cyberspace.

_____

_____

_____

_____

_____

_____

_____

_____

_____

_____

_____

Susan Sprague is a freelance writer and mother of two teenagers. She lives in Malvern, Pennsylvania.

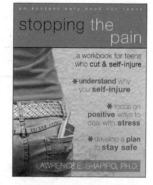